DISCARDED

The Path to School Leadership

A Portable Mentor

The Practicing Administrator's Leadership Series
Jerry J. Herman and Janice L. Herman, Editors

ROADMAPS TO SUCCESS

Other Titles in the Series Include:

Holistic Quality:
Managing, Restructuring, and Empowering Schools
Jerry J. Herman

Selecting, Managing, and Marketing Technologies
Jamieson A. McKenzie

Individuals With Disabilities:
Implementing the Newest Laws
Patricia F. First and Joan L. Curcio

Violence in the Schools:
How to Proactively Prevent and Diffuse It
Joan L. Curcio and Patricia F. First

Women in Administration:
Facilitators for Change
L. Nan Restine

Power Learning in the Classroom
Jamieson A. McKenzie

Conflict Resolution:
Building Bridges
Neil Katz

The Practicing Administrator's Leadership Series
Jerry J. Herman and Janice L. Herman, Editors

ROADMAPS
TO SUCCESS

The Path to School Leadership
A Portable Mentor

Lee G. Bolman
Terrence E. Deal

CORWIN PRESS, INC.
A Sage Publications Company
Newbury Park, California

For information address:

Corwin Press, Inc.
A Sage Publications Company
2455 Teller Road
Newbury Park, California 91320

SAGE Publications Ltd.
6 Bonhill Street
London EC2A 4PU
United Kingdom

SAGE Publications India Pvt. Ltd.
M-32 Market
Greater Kailash I
New Delhi 110 048 India

Printed in the United States of America

Library of Congress Cataloging-in-Publication Data

Bolman, Lee G.
    The path to school leadership : a portable mentor / by Lee G.
Bolman, Terrence E. Deal.
        p. cm.—(Roadmaps to Success)
    Includes bibiographical references (p.).
    ISBN 0-8039-6052-2
    1. School principals—Training of—United States. 2. School
administrators—Training of—United States. 3. School management
and organization—United States. 4. Mentors in education—United
States. 5. Educational leadership. I. Deal, Terrence E.
II. Title. III. Series.
LB1738.5.B65   1993
371.2'012—dc20   92-38985

95 96 10 9 8 7 6 5 4 3 2

Corwin Press Production Editor: Marie Louise Penchoen

Contents

Foreword

Lee Bolman and Terry Deal, well-known authors and researchers who have spent many hours working in the field of practice, begin and end this brief book by emphasizing the four decision frames that can and should be used by leaders and administrators. Between this beginning and the ending, they weave an intriguing story that demonstrates the use of these frames in practical on-site situations.

Their tale unfolds by means of a dialogue between a brand new principal, Jaime Rodriguez, and an experienced administrator, Dr. Brenda Connors, who becomes Jaime's mentor. Their discussions about the challenges of replacing a long-term, well-liked principal; about working with committees; about forgetting to compliment as well as to suggest; about numerous other real-life incidents in the experience of a new principal—all illustrate theory into practice in an exciting and realistic way.

This practical and theoretical book will be of assistance to new principals, to experienced administrators, and to any school employee who is or intends to become a leader. Applying the four frames to actual practice is an excellent contribution.

JERRY J. HERMAN
JANICE L. HERMAN
Series Co-Editors

Acknowledgments

Many of the ideas in this book were stimulated by our research on school leadership under the auspices of the National Center for Educational Leadership (NCEL), and by the work of the Harvard School Leadership Academy (HSLA), both funded under grants from the U.S. Department of Education. We are grateful to our colleagues in NCEL and HSLA for their ideas and encouragement. Many school administrators both in the United States and abroad have been *our* mentors and guides, and we have learned more from them than we can ever say. We owe special thanks to Dr. Thomas P. Johnson, Associate Superintendent in the School District of Broward County, Florida, for his support and encouragement over the long haul. Within the Bolman-Deal entourage, Homa Aminadani and Linda Corey are the logistical wizards who provide moral support for everything we do. As always, we are deeply grateful to our spouses, Sandy Deal and Joan Gallos, who make everything we do both possible and worthwhile with a perfect combination of personal support and incisive critique.

LEE G. BOLMAN
TERRENCE E. DEAL

About the Authors

Lee G. Bolman specializes in leadership and organizational change. He is the author of three books and numerous articles on leadership, organizational change, and management development, including *Reframing Organizations: Artistry, Choice, and Leadership* (written with Terrence E. Deal). Bolman has been a consultant to corporations, public agencies, universities, and public schools in the United States, Asia, Europe, and Latin America. He has taught for more than twenty years at the Harvard Graduate School of Education, where he has served as Lecturer on Education and Director of the National Center for Educational Leadership. Beginning in Fall 1993, he will be Marion Bloch Professor of Leadership at the University of Missouri, Kansas City. At Harvard he also served as educational chairperson of two executive development programs, the Institute for Educational Management and the Management Development Program. He has been director and board chair of the Organizational Behavior Teaching Society, and a director of the NTL Institute for Applied Behavioral Science. Bolman holds a B.A. in History and a Ph.D. in Organizational Behavior, both from Yale University.

Terrence E. Deal specializes in the study of organizations. He has written several books and numerous articles on organizational issues. His most recent book, co-authored with Lee G. Bolman, is *Reframing Organizations: Artistry, Choice, and Leadership* (1991). *Corporate Cultures* (1982), co-authored with Allen Kennedy and translated into ten languages, was an American bestseller and won international acclaim. Deal is a consultant to businesses, hospitals, banks, schools, colleges, religious orders, and military organizations in the United States and abroad. As Professor of Education and Human Development at Peabody College of Vanderbilt University, he teaches courses in Organizational Theory and Behavior, Symbolism, and Leadership. He serves as Co-Director of the National Center for Educational Leadership (NCEL), and Senior Research Associate at the Center for the Advanced Study of Educational Leadership (CASEL). Deal previously taught at the Harvard Graduate School of Education and the Stanford School of Education. He holds a Ph.D. in Educational Administration and Sociology from Stanford University.

Introduction

"Don't get me wrong, Don Juan," I protested. "I want to have an ally, but I also want to know everything I can. You yourself have said that knowledge is power."

"No," he said emphatically, "Power rests on the kind of knowledge one holds. What is the sense of knowing things that are useless?"

(CASTAÑEDA, 1968, p. 13)

As a school leader, you continually face the challenge of understanding what is going on and getting a handle on what you can do about it. You know how hard that is. At best, the everyday world of school leadership is complicated and fast-paced. All too often, it is frantic, turbulent, and messy. The dynamics inside your school are tough enough, not to mention the many problems and pressures that originate outside your school—district requirements, state regulations, single-interest groups, and breakdowns in families or communities.

To make sense of it all, you need to organize vague and confusing symptoms into a meaningful diagnosis so that you can choose a course of action. You draw on the experience that you've acquired over a lifetime. It's given you a set of lenses, or frames, that you use to define reality for yourself and for the people you work with. Even if your frames are sometimes wrong, you still have to use them, because they give order to confusion and let you act rather than lapse into paralysis. Your

1

frames give you strategies for responding to surprising and stressful situations that would otherwise be overwhelming.

On the basis of our work with leaders around the world, we believe you enhance your chances for success when you can use a manageable number of frames, each offering a window on different facets of the basic challenges of school leadership. The ability to use multiple frames has three advantages: (1) Each frame can be coherent, focused, and powerful; (2) the collection can be more comprehensive than any single frame; and (3) only when you have multiple frames can you *reframe*. Reframing is a conscious effort to size up a situation using multiple lenses. In times of crisis and overload, you will almost inevitably feel confused and overwhelmed if you are unable to reframe. Sometimes, when you are trapped in the wrong frame, you are immobilized. Other times, you may plunge mindlessly forward into reckless and misguided action. When we don't know what to do, we often do more of what we know, even if it makes things worse instead of better.

We have found four frames that are in common use among managers and leaders.

1. The *political* frame points out the limits of authority and the inevitability that resources are too scarce to fulfill all demands. Organizations are arenas where groups jockey for power. Goals emerge from bargaining and compromise among different interests rather than from rational analysis at the top. Conflict becomes an inescapable, even welcomed, by-product of everyday life. Handled properly, it is a source of constant energy and renewal.

2. The *human resource* frame highlights the importance of needs and motives. It holds that organizations work best when individual needs are met and the organization provides a caring, trusting work environment. Showing concern for others and providing ample opportunities for participation and shared decision making are two of the ways that organizations enlist people's commitment and involvement at all levels.

3. The *structural frame* emphasizes productivity and assumes that organizations work best when goals and roles are clear, and when the efforts of individuals and groups are well coordinated through both vertical (command, rule) and lateral (face-to-face, informal) strategies.
4. The *symbolic frame* centers attention on symbols, meaning, and faith. Every human organization creates symbols to cultivate commitment, hope, and loyalty. Symbols govern behavior through informal, implicit, and shared rules, agreements, and understandings. Stories, metaphors, heroes and heroines, ritual, ceremony, and play add zest and existential buoyancy. The organization becomes a way of life rather than merely a place of work.

If you are like most school leaders, you rely primarily on the human resource or structural lenses. The problem is that many of the situations you face are highly charged politically and deeply symbolic. If you sometimes feel that each day brings another series of ambushes and pitfalls, reframing can help.

In our teaching and consulting, we have presented this set of ideas to thousands of managers and leaders around the world. As they learn to understand and apply the frames, they regularly tell us three things:

1. The frames stay with them because they are easy to remember and to apply.
2. They see a lot things they did not notice before, things make more sense, and they feel that they finally understand what is really going on.
3. They find that when they are able to reframe, they can see new possibilities and be more versatile and effective in their responses.

In working with managers, we try to serve as guides and mentors who provide ideas and ask questions. We serve as allies in their search for knowledge, much as Don Juan did for Carlos Castañeda. Don Juan's questions and support helped

Castañeda find his own pathway. But we will never be able to work personally with all the school leaders who want to lead with more caring, confidence, and conviction. If you are one of those leaders, if you want to learn to lead more effectively, and if you continually ask yourself what you could do to make your school a better place, we wrote this book for you.

The book is designed as a portable mentor. Through a dialogue between a new principal and a seasoned veteran, the rookie comes to see troublesome situations in more complex ways, to anticipate trouble before it arises, and to develop more comprehensive and powerful strategies for leadership. Chapter 1 brings the rookie principal, Jaime Rodriguez, and a wise veteran, Brenda Connors, together. The four subsequent chapters are each built around a specific challenge facing Rodriguez in his early months as a principal. For each problem, Brenda Connors uses ideas from one of the frames to help Rodriguez get a better handle on what is happening and what to do about it.

In Chapter 2, "The Old Guard and the New Principal: Making Sense of School Politics," Rodriguez is puzzled to find that his efforts to take charge and set a direction for his school are generating a lot of opposition but very little support or appreciation. Basic ideas from the political frame help Rodriguez map the politics in his school and plot a new course toward more effective leadership.

In Chapter 3, "Sagging Morale: Responding to Human Needs," the appearance of a vicious, anonymous newsletter alerts Rodriguez to significant morale problems among the teaching staff. When he consults Brenda Connors, she guides him through basic issues in the human resource frame: individual needs, morale, participation, and empowerment.

Chapter 4, "Student Discipline: Understanding Structure in Schools," explores the often-neglected issues of the structural frame. When an effort to revise the school's discipline policy becomes hopelessly bogged down, Connors helps Rodriguez see that the revision process was unintentionally designed for failure. After the process is redesigned to clarify goals, roles, and accountability, the school is finally able to develop a policy that works.

In Chapter 5, "Celebrating the End of the Year: Symbols and Culture in Schools," Rodriguez wonders why he is still haunted by the ghost of his predecessor. Connors helps him appreciate issues of meaning, faith, and culture that are at the heart of the symbolic frame. Key members of the school's cultural network develop a powerful and moving ceremony of celebration and transition that frees the school to move forward.

The next two chapters show how all four frames can be applied to the same issue. In Chapter 6, "After the Fiesta: The Total Quality Question," Rodriguez and Connors engage in a spirited dialogue about the value of a new district initiative to create a "Total Quality Management" program. They "reframe" the new initiative by looking at its problems and possibilities through each of the four lenses.

Chapter 7, "A Talk About Values: Ethics in School Leadership," relates the four frames to ethics and moral leadership. Rodriguez and Connors explore the values embedded in each of the frames and discuss the challenge of responding to ethical dilemmas that arise when different values are in conflict.

In Chapter 8 the story comes full circle as Rodriguez becomes a mentor for another generation of school leadership. The Epilogue puts the book's lessons together in the form of a series of sign posts along the path to school leadership.

The dialogue between Jaime Rodriguez and Brenda Connors is much like those we have with educational leaders all the time. We usually offer questions rather than answers. When the questions are chosen well, they help people see things in new ways and recognize promising leadership opportunities that were there all along. When school leaders are able to reframe situations, they become more confident and more certain. They feel less anxious and overwhelmed. Most important, they are more effective and get more done.

We hope you will find the conversation between Rodriguez and Connors both lively and informative. We grounded the book in the real world of schools and in the experiences of practicing school leaders. The book offers a return to an old-fashioned approach to learning a craft. Jaime Rodriguez and

Brenda Connors do not have all the answers to the mysteries of school leadership, but they are concerned about many of the same questions and issues that are important to you. You will find yourself almost automatically applying new perspectives and insights to the challenges you face in your own job. We hope that their conversation will stimulate you to think more deeply about yourself and your approach to leadership. Above all, we hope the book will help you find new paths to confidence and success—and deepen your contribution to the students and staff members who count on you for leadership.

A New Principal Finds
a Wise Friend

As Jaime Rodriguez looked from his office into the empty
school yard, he recalled just how hard the past five years
would have been without the help of Dr. Brenda Connors. He
still remembered their first meeting five years earlier. It was in
his second week as the new principal of Pico School. As the two
of them were leaving a meeting at the district office, Connors
asked him how it was going. Rodriguez hesitated briefly, trying
to gauge whether she really wanted to know. But he had been
impressed with Connors during the meeting. She seemed to be
the kind of principal he hoped to become: caring, confident,
professional, wise, and sensitive. Averting the temptation to
give the usual pat answer, he told her, "To tell you the truth, if
I didn't have a new house and a big mortgage, I might quit
tomorrow."

Connors' response was warm and direct. "That's about how
I felt when I was a new principal. That was almost 20 years ago,
but it seems like yesterday. Would you like to go have a cup of
coffee?"

"How about something a little stronger?"

"I think I know just the place," said Connors with a knowing smile.

Once they had found a comfortable table and ordered drinks, Connors opened the conversation. "I asked how things were going because I still remember my first week as a principal. I didn't think any human being could be as scared and confused as I was and still live through it. I felt hopeless as a school leader and doubtful as a human being. But then I got a surprise. The assistant superintendent at the time was a grizzled old character named Harold Sawyer. Everyone called him 'Buzz.' He was a couple of years from retirement. He scared me at first. He seemed demanding and impatient. I got the impression that he was dumbfounded that the district had given a principalship to anyone with so little talent.

"Well, at the end of the first week, he suddenly dropped into my office late Friday afternoon. Although it seems kind of silly now, I froze. I thought he was there to tell me to clean out my desk and get out before I did any more damage to the school. I was petrified. But I'll never forget his words, 'You know,' he said, 'I was principal here for 12 years. The first six or so, I didn't have the slightest idea what in hell I was doing. If the staff hadn't carried me along, the parents would have ridden me out of town on a rail. I'm pretty sure you'll learn quicker than I did, though, so the staff won't have such a big burden. By the way, if you're interested, maybe I could help a little.'

"I'd have hugged that man right then and there if I weren't so afraid of him. I found out that he really meant it. His help was the life preserver that got me through the first year, and later he became one of the best friends I ever had. Even after he retired, we kept in touch right up until he died a couple of years ago." Connors paused, and for a moment, Rodriguez could see a trace of tears in her eyes. "I miss him. Anyway, Jaime, if you'd like someone to talk to, I'm volunteering."

"Well," said Jaime, "if you're offering a life preserver, I sure need one. Seriously, though, it's hard for me to believe that your first year was that rough."

Connors smiled. "In a few years, I'll bet there's a young principal who feels the same way about you."

Rodriguez recalled that first conversation with a smile of satisfaction. Connors' warmth and insights had been of much more value to him than the drink. She had encouraged him as he tried to explain why his first days on the job had been so unsettling. What surprised him most was that she could make sense out of so many things that were making no sense to him.

When he entered the Pico principalship, Rodriguez had felt that his most important task was to establish his authority and set high standards for both staff and students. He was also counting on the strong interpersonal skills that had always helped him build relationships, even with people who saw things differently than he did. He had once attended a leadership workshop where he was told that he was a "9-9" manager who was high on concern for both task and people. He felt confident not only that he could do the job, but that he could do it better than many of the principals that he had known. Above all, he felt excited about the contribution he hoped to make. With American education under fire, Rodriguez wanted Pico to set an example of what was possible.

But that was before his first faculty meeting. He had scheduled the meeting on the day the teachers reported back from summer vacation. On entering the meeting room a few minutes ahead of the official starting time, he was disappointed to find no one there. His discouragement grew as teachers slowly drifted in over the next thirty minutes. He was particularly offended by several who commented that they hoped the meeting wouldn't last very long.

Rodriguez opened the meeting by talking about his vision for the school. He had spent many hours working on the best way to spell out his image of a child-centered school in which all students felt that they were expected to succeed and to achieve at their full potential. He delivered his message with conviction and even fervor. As he spoke, though, he noticed that many teachers had their arms crossed. Some were simply staring out the window or at papers in front of them. After he finished, he asked for questions. At first, none came. Everyone just sat there, until one veteran teacher asked, "Shouldn't you get to know this school and how we do things before you tell us how to teach?" Rodriguez was stunned. The question felt like a direct challenge, but he was not sure how to respond.

The room felt very tense, and before Rodriguez could figure out what to say, a younger teacher, Carlos Cortez, stood up and said, with obvious anger in his voice, "The man just got here and you people don't even want to give him a chance. Mr. Rodriguez is saying things that someone has needed to say for a long time. I'm getting pretty tired of people who think this school is so perfect that we can't change anything." Cortez's outburst triggered a series of sharply-worded exchanges among older and younger teachers. Fearing that things were getting out of hand, Rodriguez moved quickly to adjourn.

The next day he got another surprise when the superintendent called him promptly at 8 a.m. "Jaime," he said, "raising standards is a great idea, but you have to be careful not to move so fast that all you do is get the faculty upset."

"Welcome to the big leagues," he thought to himself. "What's going on here?" Later he learned that right after the faculty meeting, many of the veteran teachers had held another more informal gathering at Andy's Cafe. Rodriguez had not been on the guest list. Presiding at the second meeting was Margaret Juhl, a 22-year veteran of the Pico faculty. Juhl was highly respected by most of the senior teachers, and revered by many parents in the school community. She had also served for a number of years as the representative of the teachers' union.

Rodriguez sensed that, somehow, he had got off on the wrong foot. But he was puzzled about what had gone wrong. His discomfort increased over the next several days with a steady stream of reminders from teachers about his predecessor, Phil Bailey. How many times had he heard, "That's not how Mr. Bailey would have done it," or "What Mr. Bailey would have done is . . . ." Rodriguez soon began to wonder whether he or the ghost of Phil Bailey was actually running the school.

As he had poured all this out in the first conversation with Brenda, she had listened attentively, occasionally offering a comment or question. Yet the more they talked, the better Rodriguez felt, and the more things began to make sense. He knew now what he only dimly saw then. She was offering him new lenses to help him see things more clearly. She helped him see the difference between power and authority, and the fact that new leaders always undergo some form of initiation ritual or "hazing." She reminded him that people need time to adapt to change and reassured him that being compared to Phil Bailey did not mean that he would never be accepted as Pico's principal.

Rodriguez remembered asking Brenda at the end of their conversation if they could meet again. She said, "I'd love to. I got a lot of help when I was a new principal, and now I want to return the favor." That night, Rodriguez slept better than he had in days.

The Old Guard and the
New Principal: Making Sense
of School Politics

When Rodriguez awoke the morning after his first meeting with Brenda Connors, he found himself still thinking about their conversation. He particularly remembered what Connors had said about the need to understand politics in schools. At first, he objected, "I don't want my school to be dominated by politics, and I don't think a principal should be a politician."

Connors had not challenged him directly. Instead she simply asked, "What do you make of the superintendent's phone call?"

Rodriguez was not sure what to say. He knew he was annoyed. He knew something was going on that he did not understand. He began to think about some of the people in his school. He finally said, "You're on to something. But I'm not sure how to get a handle on it."

"Well, let's try to look at this politically. Who are the influential people in your school who might not be on your side?" asked Brenda.

Rodriguez was embarrassed to realize that he had not thought very much about who was influential at Pico, or about who might not be supportive of him. He paused to review what he knew about his new school before responding, "Well, there's Sam Shepherd, the assistant principal. He was passed over for the principalship, and he's *very* unhappy that he didn't get the job. But I know why he didn't get it. He's good at cracking the whip, and he's kept the school under control. But he's almost more like a warden than a school leader. And, a lot of the black and Latino parents feel he doesn't respect their kids."

"Who else?" Brenda asked.

"There's Margaret Juhl. She's a veteran, and a lot of teachers and parents respect her. After I talked about my vision for the school in my first faculty meeting, she asked the only question, 'Shouldn't you get to know this school and how we do things before you tell us how to teach?' It felt like cold steel, a knife right to the heart. It was a very uncomfortable situation."

Brenda nodded understandingly. Then she asked, "So far, you've focused on the professional staff. Are there other people who might be important?"

Rodriguez thought for a minute. "One is Bill Hill, the custodian. Someone told me that Bill is the eyes and ears of the school. He seems to know just about everything that goes on. He's not bashful about sharing it either. It's like he's the town gossip. Then, there's my secretary, Phyllis Gleason. She goes back before Phil Bailey. She came in with the furniture. She probably knows more than I'll ever know about how the school works. I'm already beginning to realize how much I need her, but I don't get the feeling that she's very happy having me as her new boss." He stopped, and frowned. "I'm not sure if this is helping. The more I think about it, the worse it seems. Maybe my prospects aren't very good."

"Who are your allies?"

Rodriguez's hesitated for a moment. "I don't know."

"What about your younger staff?"

"Well, some of them are pretty frustrated with the way the school has been running. They think it's too conservative, that it doesn't really respond to the kids. There are three Latino teachers in the school, and I know they were glad to see me get the job. There's a young Latino teacher, Carlos Cortez, who defended me pretty strongly after Margaret Juhl jumped on me. He tells me that what the Latino teachers remember most about Phil Bailey is that he refused to do anything to celebrate Cinco de Mayo."

"What's your relationship like so far with Phyllis?" asked Connors.

"I think she's still comparing me to Phil," Rodriguez responded, "but the assistant superintendent says that she loves the school and is absolutely loyal to it."

"Maybe you should talk to Phyllis and Bill. They might be able to help you get a better picture of what's going on and what you need to do."

"What do you mean?"

"One of the things they never teach you in graduate school is how to map the political terrain. My first year as a principal, we had *big* budget cuts. Talk about a jungle! When there's a drought and the water hole starts to dry up, the animals get desperate. I realized that, in order to survive, I had to figure out who the key players were. I had to know what they wanted, and how much power they had. So I went around and talked to some people and asked some questions. Then, I actually drew a map on a piece of paper. On the right side, I put the real conservatives, the people who were probably going to resist almost any change I came up with. On the left, I put the people who I was pretty sure I could count on. Then, in the middle, I put the folks who were neutral and might go either way. There were a lot of neutrals, and that told me something right away. They could make a big difference. As I put folks on the map, I put them higher or lower depending on how much power I thought they probably had. Then I thought about how we could negotiate with each other, instead of having an undeclared war. When a new principal comes in, all the unresolved issues get opened up. The different interest groups are all jockeying to hold on to what they have and see if they can improve their situation."

Rodriguez felt uncomfortable with all the talk of power and politics. He liked to think that he was an educator, not a politician. But he had to admit that Connors made a lot of sense. "So, you're saying I need to figure out who's with me and who's against me. You might be right. Maybe I should try to draw my own map. I'll talk to Phyllis and Bill tomorrow."

While shaving that morning, Rodriguez began to rethink his idea of the principalship. His vision had always been one of presiding over a harmonious faculty intensely engaged in discussions of teaching and school improvement. This morning, he was planning to spend most of his time meeting with the secretary and the custodian. He needed them more than they needed him right now. They might be able to point out barriers and gateways on Pico School's political landscape. His old image of the principal as someone in command and on top of things was quickly evaporating. He felt both excited and apprehensive about this new course.

Whatever apprehension he had, dissipated in the first few minutes of his meeting with Phyllis Gleason. Phyllis agreed to meet as soon as he asked, though with little apparent enthusiasm. Rodriguez felt awkward at the beginning, but after a few pleasantries he got right to the point. "Phyllis, I think you can help me get a better handle on how this school really works."

She responded immediately, "You know, Phil Bailey asked me the same question in his first week here. I'm glad you asked. To tell you the truth, except for some new teachers, this place has been pretty stable for the last 20 years. You have to remember, most of these people have been together for a long time. Many of them have been friends for years, and they have a lot in common. They tend to stick together, particularly when anything from the outside threatens them."

"You mean, like me?" asked Jaime.

"Well, yes, when you start talking about high standards and about responding to children as if the teachers had never thought about those things before. In their minds, that's what they've been doing for years."

Jaime squirmed as he realized the unintended impact of his opening attempt to communicate a vision to the faculty. He listened carefully as Phyllis Gleason shared her years of experience with the Pico School's faculty and staff. Some things started to fall into place. Gleason also helped by pointing out where Rodriguez had something in common with some of the other people. He and Juhl had graduated from the same teachers' college, albeit at different times. Sam Shepherd and Rodriguez were both Rotarians. Many of the black and Hispanic teachers had been waiting for a long time for someone to champion their concerns about the education of minority kids.

Later that morning in the school's maintenance office, Bill Hill confirmed much of what Gleason had told him, but added even more. Hill had grown up in the local community and knew many of Pico's parents. He was also very well acquainted with local community leaders; three of his friends were on the district's school board. He also knew most of the students at Pico. He was in the cafeteria every morning talking to the "free breakfast" students, and served as a kind of big brother for many of them. As they talked, Rodriguez learned how much Hill loved the school. He saw himself as much more than a custodian. At the end of the meeting, Hill gave Rodriguez the names of some parents who might be willing to host an informal coffee hour to help Rodriguez get better acquainted with the community.

As Rodriguez reflected on the morning, he was surprised at how productive it had been. He told himself that he should have known better, but had not anticipated how much Gleason and Hill appreciated the feeling of being recognized and valued. Both cared about the school, and both were delighted to be treated as if they had something to teach their new principal. Rodriguez felt a little less overwhelmed. He felt he had made two allies and looked forward to reaching out to others in the school who might not be so receptive. He particularly began to think about Margaret Juhl.

Later that week, Rodriguez realized he had been right about one thing: Margaret Juhl was, initially, anything but receptive in their first one-on-one meeting. In a conversation over breakfast, she had been downright blunt. "I'm close to retirement," she said, "and I just don't have much interest in breaking in another new principal who doesn't know what he's doing. The one thing Mr. Bailey had going for him was that he usually left us alone and let us teach. He did not charge in with sermons that insult our professionalism. Let me add that I am the Pico representative for the teachers' union. At the rate you're going, you could be looking at a lot of grievances. For a new principal, that won't make your life easier."

Rodriguez's first impulse was to snap back, or to look for a way to speed up her retirement. But he remembered some counsel from Brenda Connors: "Very few school leaders know how important it is to learn how to facilitate your opposition. Why? Because otherwise, they agree to your face and then subvert you when you're not looking." Rodriguez figured this was as good a time as any to try to follow Connors' advice.

"What do you think we can do together to improve our school?" he asked.

"In the first place," she responded, "it's not *our* school. A good start would be for you to get a little more experience before assuming that you know more than everyone else."

Rodriguez winced, and tried again. "I think you're right about the sermon. I didn't know it then, but now I understand that people felt I was talking down to them. I realize I didn't get off on the right foot. I also know that I don't have all the answers. Frankly, that's why I wanted to meet with you. I need your help. Not just for my sake, but for the sake of the school and the kids. We may differ on some things, but everyone tells me how much you care about Pico and about the students. I think we agree on that, and that's why I'm hoping we can work together."

"To be honest, my first impulse was to make your life miserable. But you're right, I do care about this school. The big question for me is whether your actions are going to match your words. If they do, I'm willing to give you a chance. Since we both graduated from the state university, I suppose I ought to try to do something to help."

As the discussion continued, the climate was strained, at times even strident. But Rodriguez continued to listen and probe her views of where the school had been and where it needed to go. At the end of the conversation, he was not sure that he had a reliable ally, but Juhl seemed less interested in leading the opposition. She confirmed that at the end of the conversation when she warned him about Sam Shepherd; she even offered some hints for how Rodriguez might approach a conversation with his assistant principal. It was clear that Juhl had little respect for Shepherd, and felt that he was a negative force in the school. "Don't forget," she said, "He's only two years from retirement."

The next day, a meeting with Sam Shepherd ended when Shepherd walked out of the meeting and slammed the door behind him. Rodriguez knew that Juhl had been right. Shepherd had not said much, until Rodriguez asked for his support. Then he snarled that he'd rather consort with the devil and that he wanted no part of turning a well-run school over to the inmates.

As the door slammed, Rodriguez realized he had to do something: everyone would be better off if Shepherd moved on. Before his next meeting with Shepherd, Rodriguez did his homework. He touched base with Phyllis Gleason and Bill Hill to learn as much as he could about Shepherd. At an informal meeting with parents, he listened to parents' complaints about Shepherd's rigid and authoritarian approach to students. Even more important, he had a long talk with Margaret Juhl about Shepherd's agenda. A week later, when Shepherd walked into their second meeting, Rodriguez got right to the point. "I know you don't like me very much."

"You said it, I didn't," Shepherd muttered.

"As far as I can tell, you think the school is not big enough for both of us," Rodriguez continued. "I agree, and so does the superintendent. We want to offer you some new possibilities. I have a memo for you that lays out two options. Option one is that you move to Hillview as Assistant Principal there. It's your neighborhood, and you might find the principal and the kids there more to your liking. But you might like the other option even better. The district is willing to offer you a special arrangement for early retirement. I'm pretty sure it would give you the down payment on the hunting camp I hear you've wanted for a long time."

Shepherd looked stunned. He mumbled, "I've got to think about it," and walked out, this time without slamming the door. The next day, his letter of resignation was on Rodriguez's desk.

Connors had been right, thought Rodriguez to himself. You need to map the political terrain of an organization before making your move. Someone's position on the organizational chart does not necessarily tell you how much they know or how much influence they have. He thought back to something he'd read about sources of power, and it suddenly made sense. Some people at Pico, like Phyllis Gleason, had power, because of their information and know-how. Others, like Bill Hill, were influential because of their friends and allies. Sam Shepherd was powerful because of his control of rewards and his ability to coerce. Phil Bailey still had lingering personal power based on memories of his warmth and charisma. Rodriguez himself had the potential for substantial power as a result of his influence over agendas and symbols, even though his first effort to put them into action in his vision speech had flopped. He now had a much clearer sense of what had happened, and what he needed to do next.

By going out and talking to people, asking questions, and listening, he was able to discover areas of shared interest that made it much easier to work with most of the people in the school. Building coalitions had turned out not to be as hard as it seemed at first. But sometimes, as with Shepherd, it was necessary to take decisive steps. The key was to do it in a way that did not create a martyr or a victim around whom others could rally.

Rodriguez could hardly wait for his next weekly visit with Brenda Connors. For a change, he had a triumph to report. Her congratulations felt much better than the condolences she had given him in their previous consultation. His exhilaration was tempered, though, when Connors told him to remember that winning a battle was not the same as winning the war. He felt she was probably right but wondered what she meant. When he asked her, she smiled and said, "Let's wait and see how things go from here. But remember, a school and a kindergarten classroom have a lot in common. Like an ocean, you never turn your back on them."

3

Sagging Morale: Responding to Human Needs

Things at Pico went smoothly through October and November. As the holiday break approached, Rodriguez thought that Connors might have been too pessimistic. The school was feeling more like a placid pond than a turbulent sea. But when the storm clouds gathered, it began to seem as Connors' forecast was right on the mark. What happened at Pico after the December holiday season was even more disturbing to Rodriguez than the year's first faculty meeting. He had always prided himself in his human relations skills and found it hard to believe that teacher morale would drop as precipitously as it had. The signs were unmistakable: Teachers were coming late to faculty meetings, not showing up for parents' night, or resisting playground and cafeteria duty. Rodriguez was particularly stunned by an anonymous newsletter that viciously attacked him, complete with not-so-subtle ethnic slurs. At the end of January, he knew it was time for a long talk with Brenda Connors. Swallowing his pride at having to admit that he should have paid more heed to her warnings, he called and scheduled a dinner later that week.

He and Brenda met at a popular restaurant not far from Connors' school. Over the appetizer, Rodriguez briefed her on the latest crisis. She did not seem very surprised, but made no mention of her earlier warning on the heels of his success in dealing with Pico's politics. Connors noted that sags in teacher morale following the holidays are not unexpected. Everyone feels a little let down once the holiday afterglow fades. But then she asked some more pointed questions. She started by asking, "How's *your* morale?"

Rodriguez thought carefully before replying, "Pretty bad. Maybe it's just a slump after the holidays, but that newsletter really got to me. I can't figure out why anyone would do something like that. It had to be someone on the staff. You like to think that your staff are mature professionals, but referring to me as the 'Tortilla Kid' is a pretty low blow."

"Why might someone do something like that, Jaime?" asked Brenda.

"Racism, what else?"

"I was the first black principal in three different schools, so I know something about racism. Sure, there's racism everywhere. But I've learned that if you stop there, it doesn't help very much. It's a label, not a solution. You have to go deeper to find out what's eating at people. Someone has to be pretty frustrated to go that far. Think of it this way. People are a lot like plants. Plants have certain needs, like light, water, nutrition and warmth. When their needs are met, they grow and develop their potential. If not, they shrivel and get distorted."

"If you're saying a principal has to be a gardener, I agree. That's sort of what I try to do. I spend a lot of my time trying to make sure that my teachers get the things they need," Rodriguez responded.

"How do you do that?" asked Connors.

"One of the most important things I've done is to continue a precedent that Phil Bailey started," said Rodriguez. "I'm out visiting classrooms every day."

"What do you do when you make those visits?" Connors asked.

"I always look for things that can help my teachers do a better job. One thing I learned from my course on the principalship is that my job is to be an instructional leader, not a paper pusher. I always talk with teachers about ways to improve instruction. I want them to have the suggestions and feedback they need to create the kind of child-centered school that we all want Pico to be," said Rodriguez.

"One way that people are different from plants is that they can often tell you what you need, if you pay attention. Are you giving them what they want from you?" asked Connors.

Jaime was startled to realize that he wasn't really sure what they wanted. "I don't know," he answered. "Maybe I need to find out?"

"Start by remembering that each individual may have a unique set of needs," Brenda replied. "Some of your teachers may appreciate what you're doing, because they want feedback to help them teach better. But others might be looking for a sign that you care or a pat on the back. They might not welcome what you're offering them. Someone could even be upset enough to write a newsletter in retaliation. They might be trying to get back at you: if you make my life miserable, I'll return the favor."

"But if someone is that upset, why don't they just tell me? I've said any number of times that I'm always available. I've told them to come to me first when they're upset about something I've done."

"Having your door open does not always mean an open door," Brenda said. "Someone once told me about what he called the mystery-mastery model. What he meant was that people have a tendency to protect themselves. One way that they do that is blame someone else when things go wrong. But they rarely tell the person they're blaming, because that's risky. Maybe it's human nature to protect yourself and other people from the truth sometimes. But, I've always liked the adage that if life gives you a lemon, try to make lemonade. This newsletter crisis could turn into a promising opportunity. It could provide a chance to open up the conversation between you and the teachers, so that you and they can begin to talk about what you're feeling, and what you want from each other. Right now, you're not getting what you need, and neither are they."

"You're probably right, but where do I start?" replied Rodriguez.

"When I've run into this kind of situation, I've had good luck with bringing in a neutral third party to help get the conversation going, but that might not work here," said Connors.

"Why not?"

"Because of where the school is right now. You're still new, and the faculty is pretty suspicious. They might not trust an outsider, particularly someone you bring in. It might be better if you and your teachers could take this on together. You'll need to make sure that the faculty supports and feels involved in the process."

"So how would you begin?" asked Rodriguez.

"Suppose you start by talking to some of the people you trust. Ask them what they think is happening, and how it should be approached. When you think about a school as a family, it's important to remember that you don't always have to come up with the solution by yourself. Families often work better when everyone shares the responsibility for solving important problems," said Brenda.

"I know what you're saying is right. That's how I try to do things in my own family. Somehow, I keep thinking that a principal has to take charge and show people that he's the leader," Rodriguez replied.

"Jaime, my first year as a principal I worried a lot about that. I was afraid of losing my authority and worried that teachers wouldn't respect me. So, I tried to prove how strong I was, but it didn't work. People could tell that I was insecure. I learned from Buzz Sawyer that, sometimes, the best thing you can do is to let other people know how you're feeling. If your school is a garden, you don't have to be the only gardener. Your needs are as important as anyone else's. There's another part, too. You need to separate situations in which people want feedback from situations in which they just want support and love. When your wife asks you how she looks in a new dress, she may not always want a detailed critique. She may just want some reassurance."

The next day, Rodriguez met Margaret Juhl at the mailboxes just as she was leaving school. He asked her if she had a minute and invited her into his office. After asking a few questions about her request for more science supplies, he got to the point. "Margaret, it's no secret that we have some unhappy people at the school. And you know I'm upset about that newsletter. You've always been honest with me. What do you think is going on?"

"I'm as surprised by that as you are. Things seemed to deteriorate really fast after the holidays. Some of our regular moaners started the ball rolling, but it seems like it became infectious and almost everyone is mad about something. The newsletter seemed to be someone gunnysacking you. I think it's someone who got pretty mad, but didn't feel they could say it directly. I think it's been building for a while."

"What would you think about setting up some informal meetings with small groups of teachers to try to talk about what's going on?" asked Rodriguez.

"I'm not sure. It's been a long time since we've done anything like that. Phil Bailey tried that once when we were putting in a new report card. Everyone hated the new report card, but no one wanted to disagree publicly. Informal meetings did help then. They got people talking more openly. But if we do it now, I don't think you should initiate it."

"Who should?" asked Rodriguez.

"It would be a lot better if it came from the faculty," Margaret replied. "Let me see what I can do."

"Thanks, Margaret. Is there anything I can do to help you?"

"If you get invited to a meeting, just show up and stay cool," was Margaret's reply.

Rodriguez was surprised when an invitation came from John Leckney. He and Leckney were not close, even though Rodriguez had gone out of his way to help with some discipline problems in Leckney's classroom. As Rodriguez arrived at Leckney's home, he was surprised at how big it was. He wondered how Leckney could support a house like that on a teacher's salary. But then he was quickly drawn in by Leckney's warm greeting and hospitality. Leckney had gone to a lot of trouble to arrange the event. The real surprise for Rodriguez came after dinner. The conversation began awkwardly, as if everyone had something to say but was afraid to say it.

Rodriguez tried to get the ball rolling. By talking about what he was feeling, he hoped to get other people to open up as well. "I really want to thank John for setting up this meeting. The last several weeks have been upsetting for me, and I get the feeling that almost everyone's morale is low. I think everyone knows I was pretty upset by the anonymous newsletter. But I'm not looking for someone to blame. I'm really hoping that we can talk about what's happening at the school, and what we can do about it."

After another brief silence, one of the veteran teachers responded, "You want to know what's wrong. I'll tell you. You've been here six months, and all I've gotten from you are kicks in the butt. It's like you come in every day trying to figure out what I'm doing wrong. Did it ever occur to you that I'd like to hear if I'm doing anything right?"

Rodriguez felt every eye in the room turned to him, waiting for his response. Then it came to him that he felt the same way. "I know just what you mean, because that's how I feel. I can understand how you're looking for a pat on the back, because so am I. You're wondering if I see you doing anything right, and I'm wondering if the faculty thinks I'm doing anything right."

"So we feel you're tearing us down," said another teacher, "and you feel that we're tearing you down. It's like the saying that if you feel like a molehill, you try not to let anyone else be a mountain."

The tension had broken, and there was an air of relief, even excitement, in the room as people realized that they were all feeling starved for support and encouragement. Several teachers told their own stories around this theme, and the conversation gradually became more open and more intense. Rodriguez was still startled when Leckney suddenly interrupted someone else to blurt out, "I've got something I want to get off my chest. I feel even worse than all these other people. You made me look like a wimp in front of my students. That's why I put out that newsletter."

Rodriguez felt a rush of feelings: a mixture of anger, admiration, sorrow, and even a surprising impulse to protect Leckney.

After counting slowly to five in his mind, Rodriguez asked Leckney, "But why a broadside like that?"

"Because that's what you've done to me for the past six months," said Leckney. "You seem to save all the warm fuzzies for your Mexican friends."

Carlos Cortez jumped in. "What warm fuzzies?" he asked. "You're crazy if you think he does special favors for his so-called Mexican friends. He does the same thing to us. I'm still looking for my first compliment from the so-called Tortilla Kid." Even Rodriguez started to laugh at that point, though he was not sure why.

The laughter broke some of the tension, but everyone knew that the reference to "Mexican friends" had touched a nerve. Rodriguez chose his words carefully. "John, I appreciate your honesty. I didn't like the newsletter, and I particularly didn't like the part about the 'Tortilla Kid.' Frankly, I thought the whole thing was a cheap shot. But it took guts for you to tell me that you did it. And I hear what people are saying—that I've been making your lives miserable, and you've found ways to return the favor. We've been working on two different wave lengths. You felt that I was trying to catch you doing something wrong. All I was thinking about is how can we make this school even better."

"Well, I care about that, too," replied Leckney. "But feeling like all I get is criticism doesn't help me teach better."

"I know how that feels. I understand that I haven't been telling you about all the good things that you're doing with your students. What I'm learning tonight is that we all want a place where we feel accepted and cared for. We have some work to do to create that kind of family. Even though some of us are Latino, some are black, some are Anglo, we're all professionals, and we all have the same job to do. If we work together, we can do it."

The telephone rang later that night in Brenda Connors' home. An exhausted but elated Jaime was on the other end of the line. "Thanks," he said. "You gave me the nudge I needed. The biggest thing I learned was how big a gap you can have between what you think you're doing, and what your teachers think you're doing."

"I had to learn that the hard way myself," Connors replied. "But I got an idea that helped from a course I took once. One of the readings said that everyone has both an espoused theory and a theory-in-use. The espoused theory is the way you see yourself, and the theory-in-use is how other people actually see your behavior. What really hit home to me was that gaps between the espoused theory and the theory-in-use are the rule more than the exception. But the only way you can find out is to get honest feedback from others."

"That's exactly what happened for me," said Rodriguez. "Did the book also say that feedback can hurt?"

"Sure. That's why people don't always ask for it. But it's a case of pay now or pay later, and the price can go up a lot if you procrastinate. Hearing the truth is often painful for me in the short-run, but it seems to pay dividends over the long haul."

"Well, I've already got the pain. I hope you're right that it's going to pay off."

Student Discipline: Understanding Structure in Schools

Shakespeare was right, Rodriguez thought to himself. He could not remember the play, the course, or the English teacher who had taught it, but he remembered the line, "Sweet are the uses of adversity." February had been Rodriguez's best month yet at Pico School. The post-holiday morale crisis and the underground newsletter had led to a series of informal meetings with faculty members. The meetings had been challenging and difficult but, ultimately, exhilarating. Morale was up. People were talking with one another, and trusting one another, in a way that no one had experienced at Pico in many years. Rodriguez was on a high. "You know," he said to himself, "I think I'm finally beginning to understand how to be a principal."

A month later, the bubble burst over the issue of student discipline. Discipline had been a chronic problem at Pico School. In the old days, Sam Shepherd engaged in a relentless effort to bring offenders to justice. He had been policeman, judge, and jury all rolled into one. When teachers sent kids to Shepherd, there was never any doubt about the outcome, and Pico had little difficulty keeping students under control. Shepherd had kept the lid on the problem, but it began to boil over once he left. Teachers began to complain about not being "backed up." Several student fights had erupted in the lunchroom and on the playground. Parents had begun to voice concerns about their children's safety.

Rodriguez knew that something had to be done. Remembering past lessons, he was determined not to try to impose his own solution on the school. He also figured that this was a perfect opportunity to get positive movement on the district's new shared decision-making program. The superintendent, Mildred Hofsteder, was a strong advocate for decentralizing responsibility and for involving faculty and parents in school decision making. Every school had been asked to establish a faculty-parent council to serve as an advisory body to the principal. Since discipline was an issue of great interest to both parents and faculty, it seemed like an ideal task for the new council to work on.

Rodriguez considered two options he could offer to the new faculty-parent council. One would be to hire an administrator to replace Sam Shepherd. He knew several aspiring assistant principals who had reputations for keeping things under control. The superintendent had offered him his pick from the talent pool. The other would be to develop a new schoolwide discipline program that would involve the principal, the faculty, and even parents and students. That way, the responsibility for enforcing values and maintaining control could be shared rather than assigned to a single "cop." Rodriguez was philosophically opposed to Shepherd's one-man SWAT team approach. He doubted that it was educationally sound and that it could continue to work in the long run. He knew many parents and faculty thought that Shepherd's approach had been repressive and arbitrary, punishing the guilty and the innocent alike.

At the next meeting of the faculty-parent council, Rodriguez described the two options. At first, he was delighted when the council voted unanimously to take responsibility for developing a new schoolwide discipline policy, but his delight was short-lived. The council quickly bogged down in trivia and conflict. There were debates between liberals and conservatives, between teachers and parents, between those who wanted a single, uniform philosophy, and those who wanted more discretion for individual teachers. Rodriguez attended every meeting, and tried to help as much as he could, but nothing seemed to work. After the meetings, he found that teachers and parents usually came to him with their complaints instead of talking to the council's chairperson, Joan Hilliard.

A few weeks later, Rodriguez was stunned when he received a terse note from Joan Hilliard saying that she wanted to resign as council chairperson. Rodriguez decided on the spot that it was time for another meeting with Brenda Connors. He met her in her office near the end of the day. As usual, Brenda listened carefully as Jaime described what was happening. She then began to ask questions. This time, she focused on the council's structure: What is the council's charge? What is its internal structure? What authority does it have? To whom is it accountable. For what is it accountable? Rodriguez soon realized that he didn't know. Nor did he think anyone else had clear answers to Connors' questions. It was a blinding flash of the obvious, but still a revelation, to realize that the council's effort might have been doomed from the start by its structural flaws.

"What I've learned about groups, Jaime," said Connors, "is that they need to be clear about four things: what they're supposed to do, what authority they have, who they are accountable to, and what they're accountable for. As I listen to your description, it sounds as if those things are fuzzy for the council. For example, what does the council think they're supposed to be doing? Did they establish any criteria that the discipline policy had to meet?"

"Well, someone asked that question, but most people felt that we could work that out later in the discussion," Jaime responded.

"My experience is that groups tend to have a hard time when their job is too open-ended. It's an invitation for them to bog down," said Brenda.

"Maybe," Jaime responded, "but I was pretty clear on what the group needed to do, and in every meeting I did my best to get them on course."

"You just put your finger on another structural issue," said Brenda. "People usually depend on the chairperson to help a group stay on course. If two people try to fly the same airplane, it's likely to crash. When Joan Hilliard resigned, she might have been sending a signal about her frustrations. I doubt that she was the only person who felt frustrated. A lot of people might be wondering who owns the decision: you or the council."

"Why do you say that?" asked Jaime.

"For example, who makes the final decision: you or them? Do you have a veto, or are you just one member of the group?"

"That's the whole problem with this shared decision-making stuff," said Rodriguez. "I'm supposed to give everyone a say in the decisions. But you and I both know that when there's a problem, the monkey's going to be on my back."

"Only if you choose to accept it," Brenda replied. "Actually, I think shared decision making is a great idea, but the hard part is getting it to work. One big problem with shared decision making, and with most structural changes, is that all of a sudden things aren't as clear as they used to be. People get confused about who's in charge of what. You're right, you can't escape the responsibility of being the principal. The trap is believing that, 'If the monkey's going to be on my back anyway, I have to control the monkey.' It's like being a parent. Your kids will have a hard time growing up if you never let them make any decisions. Sometimes they'll make mistakes, and you won't always like the decisions they make. But how else will they learn?"

Jaime immediately saw her point, "You're right. It's an important part of growing up and learning to take more responsibility."

"And," said Brenda, "what helps kids, and what will help your council, is to be clear about the boundaries—which decisions they get to make, and which ones you're still responsible for."

"That makes a lot of sense, Brenda. At the next council meeting, I'm going to clarify that for them."

"Let's rethink that, Jaime." Brenda replied. "Remember some of the things you've already learned this year. How about asking people how they see the structure and how they think it should be set up. When I faced a similar situation some years ago, I put my school through the CAIRO exercise."

"It has something to do with Egypt?"

"No," said Brenda. "It's a process for clarifying responsibilities. We jointly developed a chart showing the roles and areas of responsibility that each of us had. What you do is you pinpoint who is ultimately accountable for getting something done. That person gets an 'R,' because he or she is responsible for the outcome. Then you show how that person relates to everyone else who's involved in the process. A person who gets an 'A' has the right to approve or disapprove. Someone with a 'C' has to be consulted. Someone with an 'I' has to be kept informed. 'O' is given to someone who is outside the process. The superintendent has given you an 'R' for many decisions in your school. On a lot of those, she just wants you to keep her informed. On some, she expects to be consulted. Only in a few does she expect that you get her approval."

"That's true," said Jaime. "One place where the superintendent and I were clear was on the Sam Shepherd thing. I had the 'R', because I was responsible for the results. But the superintendent needed to be consulted on my strategy, and she and the school board had to approve the two options that we offered: the transfer or the early retirement. I made sure she was with me before I approached Shepherd."

"Now you've got it," said Brenda. "What's good for the goose is good for the gander. What works for you will probably work with your school council."

Rodriguez's next step was to meet with Joan Hilliard and ask her to reconsider her decision to resign as council chairperson. She initially resisted, saying, "It finally became clear to me that it was a no-win situation. I felt responsible for everything, but everyone assumed that you were really in charge."

"That's exactly how I see the problem," Rodriguez replied. "We need to get clear about the council's role as well as the role of the chairperson. I've got an idea about how we can do it, but I need your help."

At the next meeting, Joan Hilliard led the council through a CAIRO exercise. It was an eye-opener for everyone. It turned out that there were at least three different ideas about how the discipline policy was supposed to be developed. Rodriguez and some other members of the council thought that he was really responsible. Many teachers felt that the responsibility ultimately ought to be with the faculty, since they had to implement the policy. The parents felt that the council should be able to make the final decision. The group broke into laughter when a parent commented, "This looks a lot like the way my family works."

Afterwards, Hilliard came to Rodriguez and said, "You know what I think I learned today? I think the way the council is set up almost guarantees that it will fail. It's the wrong group to try to hammer out something as complicated as the discipline policy. The council is too big, it's too diverse, it's got too much to do and too little time to do it. In the CAIRO exercise, I realized that we have too many people who think they have the 'R.' But there are about five key people who have the most investment in this policy. I think we should give that group responsibility for preparing a draft. They could consult with you, with the teachers, with the community, and with students. Then, if I understand how this shared decision making is supposed to work, the council should retain final approval of the policy."

"I think you're right on," said Jaime. "The council is having a tough time trying to deal with everything on its plate. If we give it to a smaller group and make sure they know what their charge is, they'll have a much better chance of coming up with a policy. But we'll have to make sure they understand how important it is to get other people involved in the process."

"Exactly," said Hilliard. "Let me develop a proposal. I'll check it with you, and with some of the council members. When I have something that the key people like, I'll get someone to bring it to the council."

"Joan," asked Rodriguez, "have you ever thought about becoming a principal?"

Hilliard laughed. "Ask me again in a few years. Right now I'm having too much fun as a teacher."

At the next council meeting, Hilliard had arranged for a parent to propose a new approach to the discipline problem. The parent indicated that the proposal had emerged from a number of conversations about the difficulties the council was having. "The idea that we've come up with," she said, "is to create a task force to develop a proposal that they will then bring to us. In particular, their job is to consult broadly with the school community and to develop a proposal that is fair, consistent and workable in the eyes of the faculty, parents and students. Their proposal would come here, and we will assess how well they did the job we asked them to do. We will either approve the policy, or send it back to them for more work. Once we approve, the policy goes to Mr. Rodriguez, but he has agreed in advance that he'll support whatever decision we make."

A teacher responded immediately, "That just makes so much sense. We've been beating our heads against a wall and getting nowhere. I think it's a great idea." After discussion and some modification of the proposal, the council approved it. A task force of three teachers and two parents went to work with enormous enthusiasm. After holding many meetings with different parts of the school community, they came back to the council two months later with a proposal that was, indeed, broadly viewed as fair, consistent, and workable. The council approved the new policy unanimously, and everyone was optimistic that the whole effort was a giant step forward for the school.

The council did not stop there. One parent had commented pointedly, "We've been through things like this before with the PTA. We reach decisions, but they never happen. Someone called it the 'Pico pile,' the scrap heap of policies and programs that get approved but never really happen."

Rodriguez jumped on the opportunity in the parent's comment. "It's the age-old problem of implementation. I have friends who are managers in business and hospitals, and they talk about the same problem. After a lot of attention goes into making a decision or designing a program, people assume that it will just happen on its own. Are we clear about who has the 'R' for making sure that the policy is communicated, and who has the 'R' for implementing it? Otherwise, it might all fall into my lap."

"That makes sense," said Hilliard. "It sounds as if we need another CAIRO exercise to make sure the new policy doesn't wind up in the Pico pile. Is this something the council should do, or should we ask the discipline task force to work on it?"

Rodriguez smiled to himself as the council decided to work through the implementation issues. "I think I've helped this move in the right direction without taking over," he thought to himself. "I'll tell Brenda about it tonight."

Later that night, Brenda Connors smiled to herself after another telephone conversation with Rodriguez. "He's learning fast," she thought. "I knew he had terrific people skills, but I also figured that somewhere along the line he needed to get a better handle on structure. In fact, one of the tragedies in so many schools is principals who think that, as long as they care about people, they don't need to understand anything about structure. It was the same for me when I was a young principal. In a way Jaime is catching on faster than I did." She gave herself a pat on the back by admitting that maybe she had helped to speed up his progress.

Celebrating the End of the Year: Symbols and Culture in Schools

Rodriguez and Connors met for dinner at a sidewalk cafe on a beautiful evening in May. For Rodriguez, it was a chance to thank Connors for all her help. For Connors, it was a chance to congratulate her star pupil on a very successful first year at Pico. That done, Rodriguez turned to an issue that still haunted him—the ghost of Phil Bailey. "You know, even though I feel great about everything that we've been able to do at Pico this year, I don't understand why there's still so much talk about how Phil Bailey used to do things. It still sometimes feels as if his ghost runs the school. The one thing I'd like to do before the end of the school year is exorcise Bailey's spirit."

"Maybe what you need is an exorcism, but there's another way to think about it. Part of human nature is forming attachments. We get attached to places, to activities, to ideas, and particularly to people who are important to us. It's human nature to resist the feelings of loss that come when an attachment is broken. If you lose a job, or get divorced, or move to a new city, you feel loss. Just think about your own experience. What do people feel when they lose something they care about?"

"A lot of things," replied Rodriguez. "They feel sad, angry, confused, depressed, ambivalent, you name it. I remember what my mother went through after my father's death. It was real tough."

"Sure. A death in the family might be the biggest loss of all. But you can feel loss even with something that doesn't seem so important. Remember the caboose at the end of the train? It isn't there any more. A little electronic box does the job a lot more efficiently than the old caboose and its crew."

"But," said Jaime. "I used to love waving at the caboose when I was kid."

"That was a long time ago, but you still miss the caboose. Phil Bailey is like the caboose at Pico, and you're the electronic box. One of the things that most cultures have figured out, but we sometimes forget, is that ceremonies help people deal with loss. When people die, we have wakes, flowers, funerals, and mourning periods. When people get married, we have an elaborate ceremony."

"You think marriage is a loss?" asked Rodriguez.

"Well, there's something lost and something gained in almost any major change," said Connors. "People get married for love, and companionship, and the desire to have children, and lots of other things they hope to gain. But a lot of marriages get into trouble because people have trouble letting go of old identities and old relationships. The reason there are so many jokes about in-laws is that it sometimes takes years for people to make those transitions. Phil Bailey was at Pico a long time. It's not surprising that a lot of people still miss him. Change is a little like what happens when a trapeze artist has to let go of one trapeze before grabbing the next one. It's scary to let go, but there's danger in hanging on too long."

"Does that mean we need a funeral for Bailey?"

"Something like that," Brenda replied thoughtfully. "Even though people know that you're the principal, it's harder for them to accept you until the torch has been symbolically passed. What did they do at the school to mark Phil's retirement?"

"Nothing, actually. They wanted to have a retirement dinner, but Phil said he wouldn't come if they had it."

"That means people lost the opportunity to celebrate his accomplishments, to savor the memories, to tell stories, and to say 'thank you,' and 'we care about you,' and 'we wish you well.' "

"But Bailey didn't die," said Rodriguez. "He retired. He doesn't need a casket yet. He's having too much fun on the golf course."

"But, for many people in the school," Connors responded, "his retirement feels like a death in the family. To them, he's gone and it's a loss. They've never had a chance to mourn his loss or celebrate his life at the school, so it's hard for them to let go. If people are still in denial and have not let go of Phil, it's hard for them to form attachments with you."

"So maybe what I need to do," said Rodriguez, "is plan a funeral, and see if we can get rid of the ghost for good."

"But remember, you're still a newcomer to the school's culture. You need to check in with the key people in Pico's cultural network," said Connors. "They have to be in charge of something this important."

"Who do you have in mind?" asked Rodriguez.

"What's Bill Hill's role in the school?" asked Connors.

"He's the custodian, of course."

"But isn't he a lot more than that?"

"Sure, that's one thing I've learned. Bill Hill is the eyes and ears of Pico, and he's also the unofficial message center," said Rodriguez. "I get the point. I need to talk to him, and I also need to talk to Phyllis, because she's the school historian."

"She may be even more than that. She might be the unofficial priestess of Pico School," said Brenda.

"What do you mean?" Rodriguez asked.

"From what I understand, Phyllis takes confessions and gives blessings. She keeps confidences, so she doesn't divulge what people tell her. But she weaves what she hears into her portrait of what the school is all about. She's the one who blesses things that are successful and provides comfort when things go wrong. She may be a lot like the priests and priestesses in traditional cultures. They were the storytellers, they were in charge of the tribe's rites and ceremonies. She may be a key custodian of Pico's culture."

"The way you're talking, it sounds as if I'm more like a tribal chief than a school principal," protested Rodriguez.

"You've got it," said Brenda. "And a good tribal chief, particularly a new one, knows that the tribe's spiritual leaders have to be in charge of important ceremonies. Talk to Phyllis. Ask her who should preside over your end-of-the-year ceremony. She knows the protocol. Otherwise, you might shoot yourself in the foot."

The next morning, as Rodriguez lingered over his second cup of coffee, he felt apprehensive and even a little foolish about his meeting with Phyllis Gleason. The more he thought about it, the more he worried that Brenda might be way off base. If she had not been right so many times in the past, he might have abandoned his plan.

When he and Gleason met, he opened by saying that he needed her help again. Then he asked, "Is Phil Bailey still the principal of this school?"

"Mr. Rodriguez," said Gleason, "I wondered when you'd ask me that. Mr. Bailey was around for a long time. Even though he had his quirks, people got used to him. He was like an old T-shirt. You're used to it, it's comfortable, and it reminds you of memories that get better and better as time passes. Mr. Bailey was not the kind of person who stood on ceremony. He literally walked out of the office on the last day, gave me the keys, and told me to send the stuff in his office to his home. He wouldn't let us hold a retirement party, and he didn't even show up for our end-of-the-year party. I think that hurt a lot of people. A lot of people have left-over feelings, including Mr. Bailey. I've talked to his wife a few times lately, and he's having a tough time with retirement. He sometimes calls his friends on the faculty to ask how things are going. They come and tell me about it, because they're not sure what to say. I think it's time for Mr. Bailey's retirement party."

"That would make me happy, because I feel I've been in his shadow all year long," Rodriguez responded.

"To be frank, you've done some things to make it worse," said Gleason.

"Like what?"

"Like the time you came in during Christmas vacation, cleaned out the old storeroom and redecorated it as a faculty lounge," said Gleason.

"But several teachers told me how happy they were to have the lounge," said Rodriguez.

"People don't always tell you everything. A lot of people did like the idea of the lounge, and you did a nice job of decorating it. There was just one problem. You threw out some things that people really cared about."

"You're telling me people thought that junk was important?" asked Rodriguez.

"How would you feel if someone went up to your grandmother's attic and tossed everything out?" Gleason replied.

"I think I understand. It just never occurred to me that anyone would miss any of that stuff. I meant it as a gesture of how much I support the teachers," said Rodriguez.

"You could have asked me before cleaning out the storeroom," said Gleason. "I could have told you what might happen."

"I've learned a lot this year, Phyllis. But I know I still have a lot more to learn. I hope you'll keep on giving me a hand."

"Since you're asking, let me mention one other thing," said Gleason. "Remember parents' night, when you sent the teachers a memo telling them that everyone would be in the gym, instead of meeting parents in the classrooms?"

"Sure. I had some calls from a couple of parents. They thought it would be a lot more convenient that way. Otherwise they have to wander all over the school, particularly if they have more than one child at Pico," said Rodriguez.

"Maybe, but it's always been a tradition at Pico for teachers to meet parents in their classrooms. That way, parents can see the children's work displayed, and the teachers can show off their classrooms. A lot of them work very hard on their classrooms, and they're proud of them. At Pico's open house, maybe convenience is not the most important thing for parents or teachers. Maybe they're more concerned about getting a sense of what it's really like in their child's classroom."

"Phyllis, have you ever seen *MASH?*" asked Rodriguez.

"Sure, why?"

"Our relationship is a lot like the one between Colonel Blake and Radar. You're always way ahead of me," said Rodriguez ruefully.

"I just try to do my job," said Gleason. "But you can't learn the ropes alone. Don't worry about Mr. Bailey. I'll take care of it, and I'll let you know what you need to do."

Rodriguez felt a brief twinge of resentment at the idea of taking orders from his secretary. Remembering Connors' counsel, he resisted the urge to remind Gleason who was in charge here. Instead, he simply said, "Thanks, Phyllis. Let me know what I should do."

Three weeks later, Jaime arrived at his office to find a flyer on his desk announcing the "Fiesta de Pico," to be held on a Friday evening near the end of the school year. The program highlights were to include, "Give My Regards to Bailey," "The New Principal's Report Card," and "What a Guy!" Rodriguez felt his stomach tighten, particularly when he thought about getting a report card in public. Would this be a celebration or a lynching? Was the priestess going to preside over a human sacrifice? He hoped that Brenda Connors knew what she was talking about, and that Phyllis Gleason would come through for him.

On a warm and beautiful evening in June, Rodriguez walked into the school's multipurpose room. He was bowled over: he had never seen the room look so spectacular. He tried to imagine where all the flowers, balloons, and streamers had come from, particularly since he had not signed any budget requests. His attention was particularly drawn to the large banner hanging from the opposite wall that read simply, "Fiesta de Pico: The Beat Goes On!" He noted with some relief that the room was not decorated for a lynching. But he was still nervous because Gleason had yet to tell him what he was supposed to do.

Just then, a familiar voice said, "Mr. Rodriguez, glad you came early. How do you like the decorations?" Gleason took Rodriguez aside and briefed him on his role in the event. "When Mr. Bailey arrives, shake his hand, smile, and then go find a seat in the back row. The first part of the party is for him. Whatever happens next, keep smiling, and act as if you're having a good time."

Rodriguez did not feel very reassured, but he had little time to regroup. A large crowd was pouring into the room: teachers, staff, parents on the school council, even the superintendent and all the members of the School Board. Just then, he was chagrined to see Sam Shepherd and his wife walk into the room. In his ear, he heard Phyllis whisper, "Go welcome Mr. Shepherd, and ask him about the hunting lodge. He's not doing so well financially. You might want to schedule a faculty retreat up there to give him a boost." He gritted his teeth and tried to follow Gleason's instructions. He was more than pleased at Sam Shepherd's warm response, and stunned when Mrs. Shepherd took him aside and said, "I can't thank you enough for all you did for Sam and our family."

Before he could regain his emotional equilibrium, Rodriguez saw Phil Bailey and his wife walk in to enthusiastic greetings from everyone. It was the kind of entrance that movie stars make at the Academy Awards Ceremony. Remembering Gleason's advice, Rodriguez went over to welcome Phil Bailey as warmly as possible, before taking his seat in the back row.

What followed caught him off guard. The superintendent, Mildred Hofsteder, walked to the podium. She asked Phil Bailey to come forward. She briefly recounted Bailey's years at Pico and then asked the Board Chairman to unveil the draped object at the back of the room: a large oil portrait of Bailey. The room erupted in a standing ovation and Jaime watched as tears streaked down Phil Bailey's cheeks. Though he felt jealous, he kept smiling and joined the crowd in the applause.

Bailey's speech was brief and emotional. It felt a little too emotional to Rodriguez, but he could see that many in the audience were deeply moved. He felt an unexpected sense of relief. He began to ask himself what it would take to get a raise for Phyllis through the district office.

Next at the rostrum was Margaret Juhl. Her job, she announced, was to give the new principal his first annual report card. "Heaven help me!" thought Jaime, though he forced himself to keep smiling. What followed was a delightfully humorous roast. Rodriguez received an E for effort and an N (Needs to Improve) for citizenship. He tried not to wince at his grade of Needs to Improve for "Opening Sermons to the Faculty," or his citation for "Excessive Zeal in Cleaning out Old Storerooms." His "C" (average) for the discipline policy felt low to him. But all that passed when he heard the summary recommendation: "Deserves promotion to Second-Year Principal."

Juhl then called on the superintendent. Three people shook Rodriguez's hand: Phil Bailey, the superintendent, and the board chairperson. Rodriguez felt a warm flush of joy, but what followed touched him deeply. The entire faculty came to the front of the room. Some of them were off-beat and off-tune, but their song said it all, "If you knew Jaime, like we know Jaime, Oh, Oh, What a Guy!"

The "fiesta" was not quite over. Joan Hilliard came to the podium to announce that the Pico School Faculty-Parent Council had a certificate to award to its principal, Jaime Rodriguez. She read it: "To Jaime Rodriguez, Our Principal. In his leadership of Pico School, may he ever be right. But, right or wrong, our principal!"

After the certificate, the hug from Phyllis finally gave Jaime the feeling that he really was the principal of the Pico School.

A few days after the Fiesta de Pico, an exuberant Rodriguez was meeting over lunch with Connors. He had taken special care to let her know that this lunch was his treat. Connors could sense the excitement and pride as Rodriguez reviewed the fiesta in loving detail. She congratulated him again on his success, and he again tried to express how much he appreciated her help. "It's getting late, and I have another meeting," said Brenda, "but I really want you to know how much I've valued our talks over this year. And I have a little something for you."

As Connors reached down to pick up the shopping bag she had brought with her, Jaime pulled out a gift-wrapped package from his briefcase. He placed it on the table in front of her as she brought out her own gift. "Jaime," she asked with a smile, "what's that?"

"Sort of like an apple for the teacher. Open it."

Connors unwrapped the package to find a book by Richard Rodriguez, with the title *Hunger of Memory.*

"It's a very important book for me," said Jaime. "The author and I are both named Rodriguez, though we're not related, and we're both Mexican Americans. He tells the story of what he went through in learning to live in this culture. You've helped me develop my own story." On the inside cover, the inscription read, "To Brenda, an extraordinary mentor, with thanks and love, Jaime."

Brenda beamed, and wiped away a tear. "You shouldn't have, but thanks. You don't know how much this means to me. Well, don't just sit there, open yours."

Jaime admired the package, then opened it slowly. His face broke into a broad smile, even as his eyes welled with tears. There were two items in the package. One was a copy of John Dewey's *Education and Experience.* The inscription read, "To Jaime: You have learned so much this year! I'm proud of you." The second was a small statue of Pico's mascot, the mountain lion, with a plaque that read, "To Jaime Rodriguez, a great friend and a great school leader, from Brenda Connors."

"You could call it recognition for the rookie," said Brenda, "but it's a lot more than that. It's a symbol of what you mean to me, and what I know you'll become."

After the Fiesta: The Total
Quality Question

The afterglow from the Fiesta de Pico lingered well into the summer. Rodriguez and Connors saw each other at various administrative meetings and usually met after each meeting to debrief. Talking helped both of them sort out the central office mandates that were really important from the trivia that could be postponed or ignored. Though neither of them liked spending most of the summer at work, they appreciated the time to plan and reflect before September brought another endless series of brush fires.

On a muggy July evening, they were debriefing an in-service for principals in which Thom Jensen, the associate superintendent, had pushed the district's new Total Quality Management (TQM) program.

"You know, Brenda," Rodriguez began, "Jensen made a lot of sense. TQM could be a great thing for Pico. I still don't like everything I see at the school. Some of the faculty are still defending the way they've always done things. The world has changed, the students have changed, what we know about teaching and learning has changed. I'm excited about what

TQM could do for us in taking another step forward. Of course, I know it's going to be a tough sell to the faculty, even though it's a board mandate."

"Good God!" Connors gasped. "It's not enough that we've been asked to create school councils, spend more time evaluating teachers, institute a new drug program, deal with the national goals, and work more closely with business. Now TQM? Come on! Maybe I'm getting too old for this sort of thing, but isn't this just another example of old wine in new bottles? Besides, I just read that business is starting to sour on it. Why are they trying to foist it on us?"

Rodriguez was surprised at the intensity of her reaction. "Wow!" he said. "That's the strongest reaction I think I've ever heard from you. What makes you so negative about TQM?" asked Jaime.

"To tell the truth, I haven't really looked at it that closely. But in 20 years as a principal, you see a lot of things come and go—alternative this, new that, authentic something else. A lot of today's reforms are just trying to copy whatever was hot a couple of years ago in business, just about the same time that the business people are moving on to something else."

"I know that the fad of the year is a big problem in education, Brenda. My staff keeps reminding me that the school has its Pico pile filled with all the new ideas and programs that fell by the wayside. I know TQM won't solve all our problems," Jaime responded. "But how about if we kick it around a little before giving up on it?"

"Fair enough," said Brenda. "What do you like about TQM?"

"Start with the first word, total. What I think that means is that everyone has to be involved and committed for the long haul, years really. TQM puts a big emphasis on continuity."

"Yeah, but that's what scares me," said Brenda. "In education we keep coming up with new programs like this every year. Each one is really new, and it's always touted as much better than what we did before. How do you ever get continuity if you keep throwing out what you did last year and trying something different? How is one more fad going to give us continuity?"

"I worry about that myself. That's just what happened with the quality circle fad that hit industry a few years ago. Lots of companies set up these little groups that were supposed to meet and come up with ideas to improve quality. The problem is that they were just 'installed' onto an existing system. I'm reading this book on TQM by a guy named Sashkin. What he says is that tacking quality onto the old system is like slapping a donkey's leg on an overweight cow in the hopes of giving the cow more support."

Brenda smiled at the image. "That's just what I was saying. My school has a couple of donkey's legs right now that aren't doing much to support the cow. You're going to have to do more to convince me that this isn't one more flash in the pan."

"Well, I think you have to look at the rest of the TQM idea. The other key words are quality and management. First, you've got to figure out what quality is. One thing you have to do is to figure out how to measure it. Another thing is figuring out what quality means to the customer. That's tough because it forces you to think about who your customer is. In education, we usually define quality in terms of whatever the professionals think it is, and then we try to measure it with tests that none of us really believe in anyway."

"We may not believe in those scores, but we're sure under a lot of pressure to get them up," Brenda replied.

"And that's where we paint ourselves into a corner. In business, TQM involves finding out from the customers what they want. You define quality in the eyes of the customer and then make sure that that's what you're providing."

"But who's the customer?" asked Brenda. "Isn't that part of the problem? We've got parents, kids, community, business, the central office, the board, the state, the feds, you name it. In education are you ever going to be able to get agreement about who the customer is?"

"There's no easy answer, but isn't that the kind of question we should be asking ourselves? It's a great question for the shared decision making process: Who's the customer?"

"And even if you figure that one out," protested Brenda, "how are you going to get any agreement on what quality is?"

"People may not be able to define quality, but I think a lot of the time they can recognize it when they see it. Part of our job is giving them opportunities to see what kids are producing and what they're becoming."

"I'm with you there, because the whole idea of authentic instruction makes a lot of sense to me," Connors replied. "But what does another movement add?"

"Instead of thinking of it as another movement, maybe it's a chance to tie all these things together and to get to the bottom of what all the fads have tried to do. You're right, what we're all dealing with is layers of history, the school is a trash heap full of all the stuff that comes in and gets tossed out, but it's still lying around. It's confusing, and it detracts from quality rather than improves it. That's where TQM gives us a way to put together a lot of things that we've been talking about all year. It's a philosophy that we can stay with over the long haul, instead of jumping on every new educational bandwagon that comes along."

"I've heard this song before, Jaime. What's so special about TQM that makes it different from the other movements?" asked Brenda.

"I think it incorporates the lessons I learned from you this past year. You showed me a way to look at things from different directions. One direction is in terms of your human resources—the importance of listening to people, involving them, helping them develop. A key piece in TQM is involving people and giving them the training they need so that they can be successful. There's a lot of emphasis on using task forces to figure out what quality is, to understand how the system is working, and how you could change the system instead of blaming individuals for not doing their job."

"When you talk systems, aren't you talking more about the structural side than the people?" asked Brenda.

"Well, that's the beauty. You helped me see that they're both important. TQM pushes you to do your homework and analyze your system. It also says that your suppliers are part of your system. Teachers gripe a lot about parents and how they're letting us down by sending us defective materials. TQM says bring them in and work more closely with them."

"That's the best point that you've made so far," said Brenda, her voice sounding a little less skeptical. "Working more closely with parents and families is one of my passions."

"It's starting to be one of mine, too. Instead of just pointing fingers, and keeping parents at arm's length, there are a lot of things we can to do reach out and pull them in. TQM says that you have to measure quality at three points in the process: when supplies arrive, during the process, and when you deliver to your customer. In education, we mostly measure things at the end. If the results are bad we find someone to blame, but that doesn't really help anybody."

"What you're saying makes all kinds of sense, but you're not talking superficial change here. You're talking about big changes in how we think and what we do. Aren't you talking about a cultural change?" asked Brenda.

"That may be TQM's biggest strength. Underneath it all is a philosophy and a set of values. There's the idea that quality becomes a way of life. It's what Ford is talking about with quality is job number 1. The idea is that, day in and day out, quality is part of everything that we do."

"But you can't install a culture like you put in a new computer," Brenda protested. "Again, it's like a lot of the other things that come and go. The ideas sound fine, but when you're putting together a quality program, other people will be putting together the artillery to try to shoot it down."

"You're right, you're right. I still remember what you taught me about understanding the politics. That's probably the biggest obstacle to TQM. I don't know how much the quality gurus have really thought about the political issues. It's a lot like my first day at Pico. I had the answer. In fact, quality was a key part of what I was trying to get people to buy. But the way I said it mobilized more opposition than support. My staff is tired of things being shoved down their throats, even if they make sense. Being against quality is kind of like being against motherhood, but motherhood has been a wolf in sheep's clothing before. People want to know what's under the surface."

"Will they be thinking, 'Here we go again'?" queried Brenda.

"Sure, and they'll be right. Sashkin talks about the seven deadly sins of organizations, and our district has most of them. We don't focus on the long term, we don't do enough to develop our people, and we emphasize short-term measures of successes. We spend a lot of time on teacher evaluation without accomplishing much. TQM may not be a magical cure, but it has a lot going for it."

"You know, Jaime," Brenda laughed, "you have a way to go before turning me into a TQM groupie, but I notice something else about this conversation. Our relationship is really changing. Just listen to yourself. You're becoming the teacher, and I'm learning from you."

"You know, Brenda, that means more to me than I could ever tell you. The past year I may have walked in Phil Bailey's shadow, but I also felt a lot of times that I was overshadowed by you. You were the guru and I was the wet-behind-the-ears pupil. That wasn't my idea of what principals are supposed to do."

"That's where I saw it differently. I always felt we were both learning, particularly as you started to get your feet on the ground. It's like my conversations with Buzz Sawyer. It wasn't very long before he and I became real colleagues. We both know that principals are caught in the middle; we feel it every day. It's hard for us to be completely open with teachers or with the district office. Most principals don't really seek each other out as colleagues. We've been lucky. We like each other, we enjoy being together, and we both learn. The only advantage I've had is more experience. I always liked the lyrics from a country song that goes something like this: 'I've got a couple more years on you. More chances to fly, more places to fall. It's not that I'm wiser. 've just had a couple more times with my back to the wall.' "

Both of them realized that something basic had shifted in their relationship. Rodriguez still had great respect and appreciation for everything Connors had contributed to his first year at Pico, but he no longer felt like a nervous and unseasoned beginner sitting at the feet of an all-knowing master. Rodriguez knew he still had much to learn, but for the first time he was enjoying the warm feeling of comradeship that grows between two people who value one another as both colleagues and friends.

A Talk About Values:
Ethics in
School Leadership

Rodriguez and Connors met again a week before school opened. Knowing how hectic their schedules were, they decided to schedule a regular Wednesday breakfast. Rodriguez argued that teachers traditionally viewed Wednesday as "hump day" because they were getting over the hump for one more week. He and Connors agreed to keep their mid-week meeting sacred. They both knew how easily principals' calendars get pushed around by the crisis of the day. They had created a kind of two-person support group that served as a vital nourishment for mind and spirit. They were gradually deepening their conversations by grappling with issues that principals rarely talked about.

On this particular Wednesday in late August, Rodriguez wanted to talk about ethics. He had grown up in a family that put a strong emphasis on doing the right thing. His parents always had clear answers to every question of right and wrong. Now that he was a school principal, things were not nearly so clear. "Somewhere I heard that the difference between management and leadership is that managers do things right, and leaders do the right thing," he mused. "That makes sense to me, but how do you *know* what the right thing is?"

"Doesn't it come down to what you believe in, and what your values are?" asked Connors.

"Yeah, sure, but that's what I'm trying to sort out," replied Rodriguez. "It's easy to say that I'm committed to education for all children, and it's true. I really believe that. But I've been thinking about some of the really tough situations I was up against last year. I'm beginning to think that what made them so hard was I was trying to sort out conflicting values."

Brenda smiled. "You figured that out a lot quicker than I did when I was a young principal. Somewhere along the line I learned that you have to know the difference between a *problem* and a *dilemma*. Problems have solutions. If you get the right idea or the right information, you can find an answer that is more efficient or works better. Like when you restructured the approach to the discipline problem. The process was stuck, and setting up the task force got it unstuck."

"Dilemmas are different. They don't exactly *have* solutions, because you're caught between different values. Think about all the heat at last week's school board meeting over the policy on condoms for students. You don't want to encourage teenage promiscuity, but you don't want kids dying from AIDS either. In cases like that, you have to make a value judgment. The key for me is to get clear about what values are at stake and then try to sort out how to weight them."

"That fits perfectly with this article I read in the school board journal," said Jaime with excitement. "It talked about four values that are important in education. Let's see, the four were excellence, caring, justice, and faith. I like all of them, but sometimes they're in conflict."

"Those value conflicts are the toughest things we wrestle with as principals," Brenda responded. "That's when it gets real hard to tell the difference between a ball and a strike. It's like shifting from being an umpire to being a philosopher. That article sounds interesting. Tell me more about it."

"Well, the first value, excellence, is one that we hear about all the time. Everyone is for it these days. A major part of what schools are asked to do is to help kids achieve as much as possible. In terms of that value, the role of the leader is like an engineer or an architect—diagnosing how things are working, and figuring out how to do things better."

"I'm all for excellence, but I worry when that's the only thing people focus on. A school is not a factory. We're dealing with people, not widgets," Connors responded.

"That's why the second value on that list is caring. It's the whole idea of schools as families, that people have an obligation to care about one another and to look out for each other's welfare. At its deepest, it's the whole issue of love," said Jaime.

"I like that. It fits with the idea of the leader as servant—that my job is to understand people's needs and concerns, and to serve them as well as possible by building a caring community."

"But then sometimes you run into a conflict between caring and excellence. Maybe that's what I was wrestling with in dealing with Sam Shepherd. On the one hand, excellence meant doing what was best for the students, which meant getting Sam out of his job. But, even though I didn't like what he did with kids, I still wanted to treat him with respect. I didn't want to hurt him, and if I had, it would have set a bad example for everyone else. I was caught between caring and excellence, and I had to find some way to balance them," said Rodriguez.

"That's exactly what you did," Brenda responded. "But where does justice fit in?"

"Well, as I understand the article, the basic idea of justice is fairness. It's like the statue of the blindfolded goddess with the scales," replied Jaime. "People have a right to fair and equal treatment. In dealing with Shepherd, it was important to be fair to him and to the students."

"That makes sense. Maybe the newsletter is another example. You felt that people didn't care about you, and they felt that you didn't care about them. Maybe the deeper issue wasn't caring but justice: they didn't feel that you were being fair. Like when Leckney said you were favoring the Chicano teachers."

"I never thought about it that way before," said Jaime. "But in the meeting at Leckney's house, we started off talking about caring, but later on we got into fairness. Were members of some groups being treated more favorably than other people? These things are really complicated. It's like everything is layered on top of something else, and a lot of times different layers are pitted against each other."

"Was that true for the discipline issue, too?" asked Brenda.

"Probably. On the one hand, we were trying to do what's best for children, so it was an issue of excellence. But we were also trying to balance the interests of teachers, parents, kids, and so on. It wasn't going to work unless people felt that the process and the product were fair."

"But I think there's even another layer. Maybe this is where that fourth value comes in. If you look at it symbolically, the whole process was a ceremony in search of a cultural anchor for your school community. You wanted something that everyone could believe in. So the search for justice was also a search for faith."

"In a way, that's what my whole first year was about," said Jaime. "That's really what I think I was trying to do with my vision speech last Fall—give everyone something to believe in. Where I went wrong was acting like a missionary who didn't have to pay any attention to the natives' existing faith. Teachers need to believe that they really can make a difference. We both know a lot of teachers who burned out somewhere along the line. Education is so tough and so intangible. It's hard to keep the faith, particularly when so many people are bashing schools and teachers. I cringe every time I hear someone say, 'I'm just a teacher.' We used to be proud of our profession. Now, sometimes we just feel embarrassed."

"The longer I've been a principal, the more I'm convinced that a principal has to be a spiritual leader. We have to help people recapture the meaning of the work, and we have to talk about the things that touch their hearts. Remember the Fiesta de Pico? I don't know if you knew it or not, but I came and sat in the back of the room. When the Pico faculty anointed you as their new principal, I got goose bumps. When you're dealing with a generation of children in a school, every day should give people goose bumps.

"It's like the time," Brenda continued, "when I was thinking about leaving the teaching profession. I had actually agreed to go to work for a textbook company, and I was going to hand in my resignation the next day. As I was leaving the school, a sixth-grader walked up to me and said, 'Miss Connors, you're my sister's favorite teacher this year. I'm going to be a seventh-grader next year. Will you be my teacher too?' I got a lump in my throat, and then I said, 'Yes, Katie, I probably will be your teacher.' I went back home that night and tore up my resignation."

"That story gives *me* goose bumps," replied Rodriguez. "Keeping the faith is the soul of the profession. Those other values—justice, caring, and excellence—are all important. But they won't mean much unless we really believe in the kids and believe that this is a spiritual mission."

"Right on, Socrates," said Connors with a smile. "This has been a wonderful conversation, but it's probably enough for one breakfast. I have to get to a meeting over at my school. See you next Wednesday."

Five Years Later:
Passing the Torch

It was Rodriguez's fifth year as a principal, and once again he found himself attending the first principals' meeting of the new school year. While the associate superintendent was discussing new district policies, Rodriguez's mind began to wander. His thoughts floated over Pico's past five years. Being recognized as a school of excellence had been enormously satisfying to everyone at the school, but he felt even more gratified at how far he, the staff, and the community had come over those years. Just then, his thoughts were interrupted when the associate superintendent asked, "Why are you smiling? Is there something funny about this policy?"

"I guess I was admiring all the work you put into it," Jaime responded. The associate superintendent droned on, and Rodriguez returned to his memories. This time he thought about Brenda Connors and what an important force she had been in his career. Connors had retired and moved to Florida, and Rodriguez often thought about how much he missed her. If she had been there, he would have expected a note under the table complimenting him on his quick recovery. He thought about how much of her wisdom had been incorporated into his own philosophy. Just then, his eyes wandered down the table to Sandy Dole, who had just been appointed principal of an elementary school. She was not smiling. She looked as if she was losing a difficult struggle to follow every word in the associate superintendent's presentation. More than anything, she seemed downright scared. He wondered whether she was feeling the same way he did five years ago.

At the end of the meeting, he made a special point of pulling her aside. He introduced himself and asked her, "How's it going?"

She paused, gulped, and stammered. "You want the truth? I'm not sure I'm even going to survive the week."

Jaime felt a wave of nostalgia. Smiling warmly, he said, "I remember feeling the same way my first year as a principal. How about a cup of coffee?"

Epilogue:
Diagnosis and Action
Signposts on the Path to Leadership

The dialogue between Connors and Rodriguez offered signposts along the road to leadership. They are not rules, but guides to the artistry of effective leadership.

SIGNPOST 1
Map the Politics and Follow the Map

Connors suggested three key questions to use in mapping the political terrain in a school:

1. Who are the key players? (Who are the people, or groups, who care about the issue at hand? Will they care enough to support or oppose you? Who will, or might, make a difference in how things turn out? Whose help is necessary? Whose opposition is too important to ignore?)

2. What is the interest of each of the key players or groups? (That is, what stake does each key player have in this issue? What does each player want, and what can you do to help them get at least part of what they care about?)
3. How much power does each player have? (Who is likely to have the greatest influence over how this issue turns out? What is the source of power for each key player? Who could help if their power was mobilized? Are there any "sleeping dogs" better left undisturbed?)

The answers to those questions make it possible to draw a map: a two-dimensional figure in which the vertical axis represents power and the horizontal axis represents position, or interest.

With the map in hand, it's then possible to employ the strategies of effective and constructive politicians.

1. Clarify your agenda. (You are clear on your agenda when you have both a vision of where you want to go, and a strategy for getting there.)
2. Build relationships and alliances. (Work on building relationships with the key players. Spend time with them, and find out how they think, what's important for them, and what they would like from you. The better your relationships, the more likely you are to build support and defuse opposition.)
3. Facilitate the opposition. (Talk to potential opponents. Listen to them, and ask questions to make sure that you really understand how they think and what they care about. Acknowledge the importance of their perspectives. Encourage them to engage in a dialogue with the people they disagree with.)
4. Encourage conflict. (It is tempting but dangerous to ignore conflict or to sweep it under the rug in hopes that it will go away. People need a chance to voice their own concerns, and to hear other people's concerns. Otherwise, they usually get even.)

5. Negotiate. (As you get clearer on what you and other key players want, you can engage in conversations with them about options and possibilities for "win-win" solutions. It is an ongoing search guided by the question, what can we do that works for all of us?)

SIGNPOST 2

Empower Your People

Managers often forget that individuals always bring their needs and their humanity with them when they come to work. They still need to feel safe, to belong, to feel appreciated, and to feel that they make a difference. In their eagerness to take charge and establish control, managers often make the mistake of sucking up as much responsibility and power as they can. That leaves everyone else frustrated and disempowered, while the organization bogs down because nothing gets done unless the boss does it or approves it. Connors encouraged Rodriguez to open up communications and involve the staff and community in making the school a better place. As a result, staff members felt that their needs were recognized and attended to, and feelings of ownership were spread much more broadly.

There are several things that principals can do to empower their staffs:

1. Open up communications. (Spend time with people. Listen to them. Attend to their feelings, concerns, and aspirations.)
2. Ask for feedback. (Without feedback, leaders easily become blind to how they're really seen. If the feedback is surprising or negative, listen, acknowledge its importance, and share your own feelings.)
3. Empower everyone: increase participation, provide support, share information, and move decision making as far down the organization as possible.

SIGNPOST 3

Align the Structure With the Job at Hand

People need to know where they're headed, who's in charge, what they're supposed to do, and how their efforts relate to others'. Putting talented people into a confusing structure wastes their energy and undermines their effectiveness. Structural arrangements, like human needs, require continual attention.

1. Clarify roles. (Use the "CAIRO" process. Decide who's responsible, who needs to approve, who needs to be informed or consulted, and who does not need to be involved.)
2. Design groups for success rather than failure. (Make sure that groups have a clear charge: that they know what they're supposed to do and what criteria will be used to judge their successes. Clarify to whom they are accountable: who is their client? What authority and resources does a group have? For example, does the group have the authority to make a final decision, or merely to develop a proposal that someone else will judge? Groups with manageable tasks, substantial authority, and clear accountability succeed almost every time.)

SIGNPOST 4

Celebrate Your Culture

In his opening vision speech, Rodriguez fell into a trap that snares many new leaders. He assumed, implicitly, that Pico School's culture was a blank slate waiting for him to fill it in. Every organization has a culture, and leaders need to understand the existing culture before they have any chance of influencing it.

1. Learn the history. (Cultures are created over time as people face challenges, solve problems, and try to make

sense out of their experience. The present is always sculpted by powerful echoes from the past. Frequent glances in a school's rearview mirror are as necessary as having a vision of the future.)

2. Diagnose the strength of the existing culture. (Some schools have very strong cultures: beliefs, values, and practices are clear and widely shared; people are proud of the school and its traditions. Others have weak cultures: there is little agreement about or pride in the school's identity. Weak cultures often call out for change; they are an invitation to strong leadership. Strong cultures are the reverse: they resist change and reject leaders who are seen as enemies.)

3. Identify the cultural players. (Who are the priests and priestesses? The storytellers and gossips? The heroes and heroines? Day in and day out these individuals reinforce and reinvent the culture. Priests and priestesses take confessions, give blessings when things go well, and provide solace in times of trouble. Storytellers pass on the lore and lessons of the past, while gossips keep everyone up to date. Heroes and heroines exemplify values and provide tangible role models.)

4. Reinforce and celebrate the culture's strengths. (Even in schools with weak or threadbare cultures, it is usually possible to find some things worth celebrating. Those stories, values, traditions, heroes, or heroines provide a vital starting point for updating, reinvigorating, and reframing the school's identity and culture.)

SIGNPOST 5
Reframe

1. Reframing is a deliberate effort to look at the same thing from multiple perspectives. If you start, for example, with the political frame, ask yourself, "What is going on here politically? Who are the key players? What do they want? What kind of power do they have?" Once you have a political diagnosis, ask what you can do about it:

What options are available and which seem most promising? Then, go on to other frames and go through the same process.

2. Reframing can help you steer clear of catastrophe and dramatically increase your chances for successes. Consider reframing whenever (a) a problem seems impossible or you feel completely stuck, (b) you cannot make sense of something that is happening around you, (c) you seem to encounter one land mine after another, or (d) when you are about to embark on a major initiative.

One example of reframing in action is the conversation in Chapter 7 about Total Quality Management. A second example occurs in the dialogue about ethics and moral leadership in Chapter 8. (Additional discussion of the reframing process can be found in Bolman and Deal, 1991.)

Conclusion

When he left graduate school, much of what Jaime Rodriguez knew about leadership was based on books and lectures. He was glad to have this book knowledge, because anything was better than nothing. Over the course of his career, Rodriguez was able to augment his book knowledge with wisdom that can only be gained from experience and practice. His appreciation for books, and for new ideas and concepts actually grew over time, but he also came to understand that ideas became useful only when he figured out what to do with them. This book tries to illustrate the process of converting knowing-about into know-how. In the Connors/Rodriguez conversations, we have seen a combination of reflection on and dialogue about practice. Reflection is something that readers can and should do on their own, but its value can be immeasurably enhanced with help from others—friends, colleagues, and mentors.

You know, as do we, that a book is only a partial substitute for the kind of sustained and intense relationship that Jaime Rodriguez and Brenda Connors formed with one another. But we hope that it can do some of the same things for you that Connors did for Rodriguez—raise provocative questions, offer new perspectives, challenge your thinking, and encourage your heart.

We hope that it will also encourage you to ensure that dialogue and mentoring are a rich and continuing part of your professional life. Principals often feel like isolated links in the chain of command, caught somewhere between students, teachers, parents, and the district office. Though they are surrounded and even overwhelmed by all the people clamoring for their attention, they often feel deeply lonely. They are starved for the opportunity to talk openly with someone who can really understand what their life is like. But principals can become allies and guides for each other. They can help each other through reflection and dialogue. Like Connors and Rodriguez, they can help one another create an inspiriting and elegant conversation.

In that way, they can find their own individual pathway to effective leadership. Carlos Castañeda learned from Don Juan that following one's "pathway with heart" was the ultimate challenge:

> Don Juan synthesized the rationale of his whole knowledge in the metaphor that the important thing for him was to find a path with heart and then travel its length, meaning that the identification with the amenable alternative was enough for him. The journey by itself was sufficient; any hope of arriving at a permanent position was outside the boundaries of his knowledge.

(CASTAÑEDA, 1968, p. 212)

Annotated Bibliography and References

A. General

Bolman, L. G., & Deal, T. E. (1990). *Reframing organizations.* San Francisco: Jossey-Bass.

This book presents a systematic overview of our ideas about leadership and organizations, with many illustrations and examples from schools, colleges, government, and the private sector.

Gardner, J. W. (1989). *On leadership.* New York: Free Press.

If you could read only one book on leadership, this would be a very good choice. Gardner packs a lot of wisdom and experience into a highly readable and valuable book.

B. Power and Politics

Kotter, J. P. (1985). *Power and influence: Beyond formal authority.* New York: Free Press.

This book is written for corporate managers, but school leaders will still find it very useful. It is provides a very clear and comprehensive discussion of power and politics in organizations. Kotter's discussion of the "power gap" in administrative jobs, and his chapters on managing your boss, are invaluable.

C. Responding to Human Needs

Barth, R. (1990). *Improving schools from within*. San Francisco: Jossey-Bass.

This is Roland Barth at his best, offering a clear and compelling vision of how principals can work with teachers, parents, and children to build learning communities.

Kouzes, J. M., & Posner, B. Z. (1988). *The leadership challenge: How to get extraordinary things done in organizations*. San Francisco: Jossey-Bass.

A stimulating and inspiring discussion of the practices of managers operating at their personal best.

D. Understanding Structure in Schools

Galbraith, J. (1977). *Organization design*. Reading, MA: Addison-Wesley.

A short introduction to organization structure that is as readable as it is rigorous and intellectually challenging.

E. Symbols and Culture in Schools

Bolman, L. G., & Deal, T. E. (1992, Autumn). What makes a team work? Inside the soul of a new machine. *Organizational Dynamics*.

This article uses a famous case of an unusually effective design team to illustrate the symbolic and cultural elements that are critical to peak performance.

Deal, T. E., & Kennedy, A. (1982). *Corporate cultures*. Reading, MA: Addison-Wesley.

A ground-breaking best-seller that first popularized the idea of organizational culture. The original overview—and still one of the best—of what culture is, how it works, and how it can be shaped.

Deal, T. E., & Peterson, K. (1990, September). *The principal's role in shaping school culture*. Washington, DC: Government Printing Office.

A down-to-earth, practical guide to analyzing and changing school culture.

F. Total Quality

Herman, J. J. (1993). *Holistic quality: Managing, restructuring, and empowering schools.* Newbury Park, CA: Corwin.

This to-the-point book goes beyond the faddishness of TQM to show how quality management can be integrated with effective schools research, strategic planning, and school-based management. The result is a pragmatic, affordable, and effective approach to quality improvement in schools.

Sashkin, M., & Kiser, K. (1991). *Total quality management.* Baltimore: Ducochon Press.

This is another good introduction and overview of the philosophy of TQM and the issues that managers face in implementing quality programs.

G. Ethics in School Leadership

Bolman, L. G., & Deal, T. E. (1992). Images of leadership. *American School Board Journal, 179*(4), 36-39.

This article spells out the four values that Jaime and Brenda discuss in Chapter 7, and relates them to four different images of what a school is: family, factory, jungle, and cathedral.

Brown, M. T., (1990). *Working ethics: Strategies for decision making and organizational responsibility.* San Francisco: Jossey-Bass.

Brown provides practical advice for analyzing and discussing basic elements in ethical decision making: observations, value judgments, and assumptions. He particularly emphasizes the importance of articulating and discussing differences in how people in an organization make ethical decisions.

References

Bolman, L. G., & Deal, T. E. (1991). *Reframing organizations.* San Francisco: Jossey-Bass.

Castañeda, C. (1968). *The teachings of Don Juan: The Yaqui way of knowledge.* New York: Ballantine.